VIOLENCE
AND VIDEO GAMES

By John L. Hakala

ReferencePoint
Press®

San Diego, CA

LIBRARY OF CONGRESS CATALOGING-IN-PUBLICATION DATA

Name: Hakala, John L., 1989– author.
Title: Violence and Video Games/by John L. Hakala.
Description: San Diego, CA: ReferencePoint Press, Inc., [2019] | Series: The World of Video
Games | Audience: Grade 9 to 12 | Includes bibliographical references and index.
ISBN: 978-1-68282-563-1 (hardback)
ISBN: 978-1-68282-564-8 (ebook)
The complete Library of Congress record is available at www.loc.gov.

CONTENTS

IMPORTANT EVENTS IN THE HISTORY OF
VIDEO GAMES

1976
Death Race receives criticism for its violence.

1999
The school shooting at Columbine High School in Colorado prompts a national discussion of popular violent video games such as *Doom* and *Wolfenstein 3D*.

1971
Galaxy Game, the first arcade video game, is released.

1993
Senator Joe Lieberman brings Congressional attention to violent video games.

| 1970 | 1975 | 1980 | 1990 | 1995 |

1972
The Magnavox Odyssey, the first at-home gaming system, is introduced.

1992
The arcade version of *Mortal Kombat* shows blood spatter and characters dying.

1994
The ESRB is created to establish a ratings system for video games.

2013
Grand Theft Auto V receives criticism for explicit violence and sexual content.

2011
The US Supreme Court rules in *Brown v. Entertainment Merchants Association* that video games are protected speech under the First Amendment.

2018
The school shooting in Parkland, Florida, prompts a White House meeting between video game industry representatives and President Donald Trump.

2002
The US army releases the video game *America's Army* as a recruitment tool.

| 2000 | 2005 | 2010 | 2015 | 2020 |

2001
Halo: Combat Evolved revolutionizes first-person shooter video games.

2007
Call of Duty 4: Modern Warfare is released and depicts graphic violence in highly realistic modern military scenarios.

2016
Pokémon Go helps popularize augmented reality, which some experts believe is the future of video games.

2013
The Sandy Hook school shooting in Newtown, Connecticut, prompts Vice President Joe Biden to hold a White House meeting with various professionals and organizations to discuss violence in video games.

A WORLD OF
VIOLENCE

In February 2018, President Donald Trump met at the White House with families and victims of the Marjorie Stoneman Douglas High School shooting in Parkland, Florida. The president held the meeting to discuss possible causes and solutions for the ongoing violence in United States schools. Between January 2013 and February 2018, 1,875 people were killed and 6,848 were injured as a result of mass shootings in the United States. Violent video games were brought up by President Trump as a possible culprit. He stated, "The video games, the movies, the internet stuff is so violent. . . . I have a young—very young son, who—I look at some of the things he's watching, and I say, how is that possible?"[1] While the 2018 shooting led to resurfacing questions about violence in the media, the debate over violent video games and school shootings has been argued for decades.

IMPACTING SOCIETY

Video games have stirred up controversy since the first game depicting violence came out in the 1970s. The first games were hardly realistic in terms of graphics and content, but that would soon change.

President Donald Trump spoke with students affected by the shooting in Parkland, Florida. They discussed violent video games as well as school safety measures.

Twenty-first century gamers wield a variety of weapons in countless digital worlds to vanquish aliens, animals, and people.

Popular game series such as God of War, Grand Theft Auto, and Mortal Kombat feature extremely gruesome and realistic violence. Gamers of all ages can cut off limbs or attack pedestrians with cars and weapons. They are typically rewarded by the game for doing so with points, in-game money, and unlockable characters.

Even though a rating system exists for video games, some people believe that more violent media only adds to the problem for young people and therefore violent games shouldn't exist at all, regardless of rating. Psychologist Dr. Brad Bushman compares playing violent video games to a dangerous habit. He states, "A single cigarette won't cause lung cancer, but smoking over weeks or months or years greatly increases the risk. In the same way, repeated exposure to violent video games may have a cumulative effect on aggression."[2]

Critics of violent video games believe that they cause increased levels of real-life violence. Speaking at a National Rifle Association (NRA) convention, former US Army Ranger Dave Grossman said, "It's the sick movies and the sick TV shows and especially the sick video games around the planet that are creating sick, sick kids."[3] Grossman is an outspoken and controversial critic of violent video games. However some argue that by focusing on violent video games, Grossman ignores other factors that lead young people to commit violence.

Critics also worry about negative effects on society that come from rewarding gamers for their digital acts of violence. Humans can be trained in new behaviors without realizing it. Powerful psychological training techniques are woven into video games. There is potential to learn both positive and negative behaviors.

Despite all the fears surrounding violent video games, there are benefits for avid gamers. Military and law enforcement personnel benefit from violent game-based simulations. Through situational training exercises and weapons accuracy training, these individuals are better equipped to protect themselves and the nation and communities they serve.

Video games have even displayed positive health benefits. Dr. Isabela Granic, a psychology professor at Radboud University Nijmegen in the Netherlands, says, "If playing video games simply makes people happier, this seems to be a fundamental emotional benefit to consider."[4] New research indicates action games have the potential to make people smarter. Another study reveals that when new violent video games are released, there is a decrease in violent crime in the real world.

MUCH AT STAKE

Both critics and advocates believe that many people are affected by the future of violent video games. The US Constitution's First and Second Amendments are often mentioned when discussing violent games and gun violence. The First Amendment grants the right to freedom of speech. The Second Amendment grants the right for civilians to own and use firearms. The US Supreme Court has even weighed in on the violent gaming debate.

Experts suggest moderation is an important aspect of video gaming. Even some of the biggest violent video game fans feel many games have gone too far in terms of the violence and other extreme acts depicted. Behavioral specialist Dr. Marcie Biegle states, "If people are spending hours upon hours playing video games, it has to impact their behavior in the way they act."[5]

Society is responding with new laws, scientific studies, and opinions that will shape the future of violence and video games. Has society lost a sense of morality because of violent video games, or has the world only begun to reap the benefits of these titles? While the debate over their use continues, they become more and more popular. More people than ever are playing violent video games.

> **"If people are spending hours upon hours playing video games, it has to impact their behavior in the way they act."** [5]
>
> —Dr. Marcie Biegle, behavioral specialist

WHAT IS VIOLENCE
IN VIDEO GAMES?

Arcades are places where people of all ages can pay money to play video games. They have become relatively rare today, but in the 1970s and 1980s they were extremely popular among gamers. The first arcade video game was released in 1971. It was called *Galaxy Game*. In the game, two players controlled space ships and fired torpedoes at each other. When it was released, it cost a dime for one play, or a quarter for three plays. Shortly after *Galaxy Game*'s release, the iconic game *Pong* burst onto the arcade scene in 1972. *Pong* was a simple, two-dimensional game of table tennis. People loved playing video games in arcades. Suddenly, there was a large demand to bring this gaming experience home.

Video games have been in American households since 1972. The first at-home gaming console was the Magnavox Odyssey. The original Odyssey connected to the television but was powered by batteries. The Odyssey featured two controllers that had to remain on a flat surface, such as the floor. The players adjusted controller knobs to move white lines up and down on the black background. If the games required color or a varying background, the gamer needed to stick a transparent overlay onto the surface of the television screen.

The Magnavox Odyssey stored games on game cards. However, the game cards did not keep track of a player's progress.

The Odyssey games were loaded onto game cards. Game cards were inserted into the console. Some of the game cards to choose from were *Tennis*, *Football*, *Cat and Mouse*, *Hockey*, and *Submarine*. The Odyssey console did not any have memory features. This meant players had to keep track of the score with pen and paper and could not save their progress in a game if they stopped playing.

Despite limitations, the Odyssey's technology captured the imagination of people across the United States. With games consisting of simple shapes moving around screens, players had to use their imaginations to envision the thrilling scenarios that played out in games' advertisements or box art. New technology has enabled more advanced gaming experiences. It has also made it possible to make game violence more vivid and realistic.

Fighting video games such as Mortal Kombat *or* Street Fighter II *(above) are often played by two players. They can be played at home or in arcades.*

THE FIRST VIOLENT VIDEO GAMES

While the Odyssey was the first home video game system, arcade games were the first to feature controversial violence. The first notable arcade video game that portrayed violence was called *Death Race*. It was released in 1976 by a company called Exidy.

The goal of *Death Race* was to run over gremlins with a vehicle. Some people believed the gremlins looked like humans. By modern standards, the graphics were very basic. However, the violence *Death Race* portrayed was highly controversial at the time. Shortly after *Death Race*'s arcade release, the National Safety Council, a nonprofit organization that focuses on safety in communities and workplaces across the United States, described the game as "sick and morbid."[6] But Exidy made a lot of money due to the controversy. Former Exidy president Pete Kauffman said, "It seemed like the more controversy . . . the more our sales increased."[7] It would not be long before violent games became a mainstay in many households. *Death Race* was released on the Nintendo Entertainment System (NES) in 1990.

Acclaim Entertainment's *Mortal Kombat* was first released to arcades in 1992 and at home on the Super Nintendo Entertainment System (SNES) in 1993. It forever changed the video game industry. In the game, two combatants face off against each other and battle to the death. The winning character could rip out the heart or tear the head off the other character as a gruesome trophy. Before the at-home version was released, Nintendo executive Howard Lincoln believed the violence needed to be scaled back. Acclaim's former CEO Gregory Fischbach said, "Lincoln told us we needed to change the blood from red to green, which I thought was pretty stupid."[8] But a larger change to video games was on the horizon. Fischbach added, "At one point in time, games were just meant for children, and nobody really took them seriously. But it was with the launch of *Mortal Kombat* that people who controlled the media began to look at it differently."[9]

> **"At one point in time, games were just meant for children, and nobody really took them seriously. But it was with the launch of *Mortal Kombat* that people who controlled the media began to look at it differently."** [9]
>
> —*Gregory Fischbach, former CEO, Acclaim*

The video game company Sega, which made the Genesis gaming console, took a gamble. *Mortal Kombat* was also released for the Genesis. A cheat code, or a code entered into a game to unlock bonus features or extra abilities, for the Sega Genesis version allowed users to unlock the fully uncensored blood, gore, and violence. The Sega Genesis version sold five times as many copies as the Super Nintendo version. But soon, *Mortal Kombat* caught the attention of US politicians. Author Blake Harris notes, "Bill Andresen, a former chief of staff to Senator Joe Lieberman, was asked by his son to buy *Mortal Kombat*. But when Andresen saw the game, he showed it to Lieberman, who was appalled by it."[10]

Lieberman quickly started a campaign to bring awareness to the content in violent video games. In December 1993, he showed a video to members of the press which displayed the most graphic scenes and elements from *Mortal Kombat* and another violent title called *Night Trap*. "We're talking about video games that glorify violence and teach children to enjoy inflicting the most gruesome forms of cruelty imaginable," said Lieberman.[11] He adds, "Few parents would buy these games for their kids if they knew what was in them."[12] Based on his findings, Senator Lieberman announced his intention to begin an age-appropriate ratings system.

Advancing graphics and sound technology made simulated environments and violence more realistic than ever. *Doom* was released in 1993 for personal computers (PCs). *Doom* put

> "Few parents would buy these games for their kids if they knew what was in them."[12]
>
> —Joe Lieberman, US senator

the gamer into the shoes of a marine trapped in a horrifying realm facing demons and frightening creatures. The cocreator of *Doom*, John Romero, said, "There was never a name for the *Doom* marine because it's supposed to be you."[13]

Doom was wildly popular. Despite a modest price of $9, the game reportedly made a staggering $100,000 a day in sales in the first few days following its 1993 release. An estimated two to three million copies were sold from 1993 to 1999. This was an incredibly high number for that time period. It is estimated that a free version of the game was downloaded on twenty to thirty million computers. Many parents were frightened by the violent gameplay and weaponry. Some parents banned *Doom*, but children found ways to play the game away from home or on another computer.

VIOLENT GAMING IN THE TWENTY-FIRST CENTURY

The new millennium saw a more realistic gaming experience. *Halo: Combat Evolved* was released in November 2001. This science fiction first-person shooter game put the gamer into the shoes of an armored soldier named John-117, otherwise known as Master Chief. This character's mission was to destroy the alien race called the Covenant that posed a threat to mankind. In order to do so, Master Chief leaves behind a wake of alien blood and gore. The game's graphics made the violence far more advanced than those in the *Doom* generation. Some consider the game a masterpiece by 2001 standards.

Halo was so well received by fans that it led to several sequels. The game was exclusive to Microsoft's Xbox console. Incredible sales made Microsoft a success in the video game industry and propelled *Halo*'s creator Bungie Studios to become one of the most successful

People cosplay, or dress up, as Master Chief from Halo *at fan conventions. The Halo series remains popular years after the first game's original release.*

game developers of all time. *Halo* inspired a new wave of first-person shooters that would define the next generation of gaming, such as video games in the Tom Clancy and Call of Duty franchises.

The first few games in the Call of Duty series were set in World War II (1939–1945), but the series moved into the present day in 2007. The fourth game in the series, *Call of Duty 4: Modern Warfare* features both a single player campaign and an online multiplayer option. The campaign mode featured events that were strikingly realistic, along with plausible military scenarios located in the Middle East and Russia. The weapons were even modeled after modern-day military weapons.

Warfare isn't the only type of violence depicted in modern video games. The content of the games in the Grand Theft Auto series has made them some of the most controversial games of all time. The first game, *Grand Theft Auto*, was released in 1997. The game, in which players drove cars, shot guns, and escaped from police, was played in a top-down or overhead view. This distanced the player from the violence. *Grand Theft Auto V* was released in 2013. It is a fully three-dimensional open-world game in which players can explore a huge region. The depictions of crimes such as assault, armed robbery, carjacking, and murder are very realistic. The player chooses from a variety of tools and firearms to carry out their objectives. Some players even choose to simply wander the city killing innocent bystanders or police officers. Critics argue that these games glorify and even promote random acts of violence.

Despite pushback from parents and community organizations, the studio behind the Grand Theft Auto series, Rockstar Games, continues to create more of these games. Take-Two Interactive is the game's publisher. Strauss Zelnick, CEO of Take-Two Interactive, said, "The incredible ongoing success of *Grand Theft Auto V* and *Grand Theft Auto Online* underscores Rockstar Games unparalleled skill at producing iconic entertainment experiences that attract and engage new audiences for years after release."[14] Since its launch in 2013, *Grand Theft Auto V* has generated more than $6 billion in revenue worldwide. Zelnick proudly hails *Grand Theft Auto V* as the most profitable entertainment product ever made.

Realism continues to be a goal of game producers. Virtual reality (VR) technology is pushing the bounds of realism in video games. In VR, a gamer puts on a headset and headphones. VR immerses a gamer into a computer-generated world that is manipulated or

17

changed by head and body movements. It is significantly different than looking at a television or computer screen. A gamer feels as though they are truly a part of the action.

Some game developers are frightened by what violence adds to this experience. Discussing video game death and violence, a developer for the company Guerilla Games, Piers Jackson, states, "It's more intense, you can look away from it but you can't escape it. You will feel it, like everything in VR, you will feel everything much more intensely."[15] Many game developers have avoided depicting human death in VR games because of this added intensity.

> **"It's more intense, you can look away from it but you can't escape it. You will feel it, like everything in VR, you will feel everything much more intensely."** [15]
>
> *—Piers Jackson, Guerilla Games developer*

WHO PLAYS VIOLENT VIDEO GAMES?

Video games are used by all types of people. Mobile devices, such as cell phones and tablets, have made video games more accessible than ever. In 2017, sixty percent of US households played games on smartphones or other wireless devices. Countless titles are now low-cost or even free.

Each year, the Entertainment Software Association (ESA) conducts a survey on the demographics of people who play video games.

The ESA seeks responses from more than 4,000 households. The responses help video game companies decide which types of games to make for different audiences.

In 2015, the ESA estimated 155 million Americans play video games. The 2018 report indicates that 72 percent of people who play video games are over the age of eighteen. In fact, the average age of a gamer is thirty-five. Adult women are more likely to be gamers than boys under eighteen. Additionally, adult women make up 31 percent of the total gaming population.

American households have shown to be very welcoming to video games and gamers. The ESA reports that 64 percent of American homes have someone who regularly plays video games. Seventy-one percent of parents believe that video games positively impact the life of their children, and sixty-seven percent of parents play video games with their children at least once a week. Many parents embrace the gaming world. Judy Dumontet, a Los Angeles film writer and mother of two, states, "I'm not a soccer mom. I'm a gaming mom."[16]

Fifty-six percent of frequent gamers prefer multiplayer titles. They play for an average of seven hours a week. The most commonly played genre of multiplayer games is first-person shooter, a genre that frequently includes violent content. All of this data suggests that millions of Americans play violent video games on a regular basis.

THE RIGHT GAMES IN THE RIGHT HANDS

Senator Lieberman's campaign against violent video games ultimately led the video game industry to create and regulate the Entertainment Software Rating Board (ESRB). The ESRB uses a ratings system to determine which games are appropriate for different age groups. The ESRB evaluates games for PCs, mobile devices, and traditional gaming consoles. Today, there are five major categories in the ESRB ratings: Everyone (E), Everyone 10+ (E10+), Teen (T), Mature (M), and Adults Only (AO). The ESRB evaluates video game content for violence, drug use, language, and other adult themes. According to US senator Herb Kohl in 2004, "The ratings system makes it crystal clear whether or not the content of the video game is appropriate for young children."[17]

The E category indicates that the content is suitable for any age. This category may still feature minimal violence. In *Mario Party 10*, minimal cartoon violence is demonstrated by characters shooting cannonballs at each other from cartoon tanks or bonking one another with oversized mallets. An E10+ game accepts a higher degree of mild violence, language, or suggestive themes. These titles are generally acceptable for anyone over the age of ten.

Titles that are rated T are considered suitable for gamers over the age of thirteen. These games may contain violence, minimal use of blood, and some use of strong language. In 2017, an extremely popular game called *Fortnite: Battle Royale* was released with a T rating. In *Fortnite*, players engage in constant battles using guns, swords, and grenades. Gamers can also set traps to defeat enemies using electricity, spikes, or poison gas.

Games rated M are rated for people over the age of seventeen. These games have a lot of violence, blood, and realistic gore. Some M-rated titles include *Hitman*, *Grand Theft Auto V*, and *Gears of War 3*. *Gears of War 3* puts the gamer in the role of a soldier named Marcus Fenix. He dismembers, decapitates, and slices creatures in half. There are large pools of blood and gore. In one particularly graphic scene, the characters stomp on the head of the enemy until it breaks apart. These games also commonly feature heavy use of

CONTROVERSIAL VR

While some game developers have chosen to avoid introducing violence into the VR gaming world, others have not. In 2016, the company Epic Games unveiled the game *Bullet Train*. In this title, the gamer is immersed into a train station as a gun-wielding agent. The agent quickly comes under attack by enemy forces. The gamer must master close combat with a variety of weapons to win. The environment and simulated violence are incredibly realistic.

Facebook set up a demo booth for *Bullet Train* at a political conference. The game is featured on the Oculus Rift VR headset, which was created by a division of Facebook. This conference was held shortly after the high school shooting in Parkland, Florida. Many believe demonstrating this game at that time was in poor taste. After receiving harsh criticism on social media, Facebook removed the game demo from the conference.

expletives and other strong language. In 2017, only thirteen percent of all games were given an M rating. However, six of the twenty best sellers were rated M, including the top game, *Call of Duty: WWII.*

Games rated AO are considered suited for gamers over eighteen. These titles feature prolonged sequences of extreme violence or graphic sexual content. Some AO titles also include gambling with real money. While states cannot legally ban the sale of these games to minors, most retailers simply choose to not carry, sell, or rent games with an AO rating. As a result, developers have made very few AO-rated games. Many retailers, such as Game Stop, have also chosen to restrict the sale or rental of M-rated games to players under seventeen unless they have permission from a parent or guardian. The ESRB supports this decision by retailers.

Many gaming companies such as Activision Blizzard prefer a self-regulatory rating system to government regulation. Working with the ESRB is cheaper and carries less risk to companies. But critics of the ESRB believe self-policing and lack of transparency may be used to unfairly protect or downplay the level of violence in video games.

Regardless of concerns from critics, many parents take special consideration of the ESRB rating before purchasing a game. The ESA survey indicates that the ESRB is widely considered to be a trustworthy source. In 2017, 82 percent of parents were very familiar with the ESRB ratings system. Within this group, 95 percent are very confident the rating system is accurate. Former US senator John Ensign says, "It's important that each and every one of these millions of shoppers is aware of the ESRB rating system, so they can better understand what's in a game and if it's suitable for their families."[18]

With so many households embracing gaming technology, video games have undoubtedly made an impact on the lives of millions of people. Critics of violent video games believe this is leading to a rise in a culture of violence. Popular culture, media, and other aspects of the US lifestyle are influenced by the world of video games. With such widespread use, violent games are leaving a mark on the economy.

BILLION-DOLLAR VIOLENCE

The video game industry brings in a massive amount of revenue. The ESA estimates the video game industry made $36 billion in 2017. That is an 18 percent rise from the previous year, in which the industry collected $30.4 billion. Of the 2017 revenue, $29.1 billion was collected from game software and in-game purchases. The other $6.9 billion was from hardware and gaming system sales. "2017 was a special year for the industry, and for everyone who loves games," said video game analyst Mat Piscatella.[19] He added, "From mobile to PC, and from console to virtual reality, growth was achieved because the passion of gamers was matched only by the talent of game makers."[20]

> "From mobile to PC, and from console to virtual reality, growth was achieved because the passion of gamers was matched only by the talent of game makers." [20]
>
> —Mat Piscatella, video game analyst

Two genres most commonly associated with violence are first-person shooters and fighting games. In 2016, these two categories combined made up one-third of all video games sales. Action and adventure games also commonly contain violent content. Sales trends show the market for violent video games is strong.

The 2017 top-seller, *Call of Duty: WWII*, surpassed $1 billion in sales by the start of 2018. It is rated M for blood, gore, intense violence, and strong language. The ESRB content summary for the game goes into detail:

> *Players use machine guns, shotguns, rocket launchers, and explosives to kill enemy soldiers; some weapon attacks result in decapitation and/or dismemberment, leaving bloodstains and body parts on the ground. Battles are frenetic and accompanied by realistic gunfire, screams of pain, and large explosions. Cutscenes also depict instances of violence: a prisoner shot in the head at close-range; enemy soldiers shooting themselves to avoid capture.*[21]

Fortnite *can be played on different game consoles, including the Nintendo Switch. It is a popular E-Sports game that also features violence.*

A highly anticipated game called *God of War* was released in April 2018. The ESRB reports common activities in the game include slashing, stabbing, impaling, and decapitation. Previous versions of the game were both extremely violent and extremely successful. *God of War* reportedly sold over 3.1 million copies in the first three days.

The sale and enjoyment of video games is only one important component of the gaming economy. E-Sports is another billion-dollar industry centered around video games. E-Sports are competitive gaming events. Gamers join teams and leagues for their favorite multiplayer titles. Tournaments often involve large monetary prizes for the champions. There are many E-Sports competitors that have amassed millions of dollars from competitions and sponsorship deals.

Most E-Sports games feature violent content. In 2018, the game *Dota 2*, which involves violence, was the most commonly played game for the highest earning E-Sports competitors. *Dota 2* is a multiplayer game played by two teams comprised of five players each. The goal of a team is to fight and destroy the other team's base.

The ten games in which E-Sports gamers won the most money in 2017 were all rated either T or M. Advocates for E-Sports have tried to get competitive gaming into the Olympic Games. But the International Olympic Committee has determined that even if E-Sports become an official Olympic event, titles with violence will not be considered.

As the gaming industry grows, so do the number of controversies. Violent video games have many outspoken critics, from psychologists to safety experts to government officials. Conversely, others believe that violent video games may have a positive effect on society. Whether positive or negative, violent content in video games is affecting people in the real world.

HOW DOES VIOLENCE IN VIDEO GAMES **AFFECT THE BRAIN AND BODY?**

As the lines between reality and digital media begin to blur, critics fear there is irreparable damage done to the mind and body from increased consumption of violent video games. For decades, experts have warned about possible negative effects from exposure to violent media. In 1972, US surgeon general Dr. Jesse L. Steinfeld declared, "It is clear to me that the causal relationship between televised violence and antisocial behavior is sufficient to warrant appropriate and immediate remedial action."[22]

AGGRESSIVE TENDENCIES

With violent video games entering the lives of millions of young people, psychologists and other experts have wondered whether these games have an effect on levels of aggression. The American Psychological Association (APA) created a task force in 2015 to investigate this question. It reviewed over one hundred studies conducted between 2005 and 2013 that regard violence and video games. Following their review, the APA concluded that playing violent video games creates an increase in aggressive behaviors. Task force chair Mark Appelbaum reinforces this conclusion by stating, "The link between violence in video games and increased aggression in players is one of the most studied and best established in the field."[23] The study does not find a direct link between violent video games and acts of criminal violence. However, the APA determined that the use of violent video games is one risk factor in driving someone to violence and aggression.

> **"The link between violence in video games and increased aggression in players is one of the most studied and best established in the field." [23]**
>
> *—Mark Appelbaum, Chair of the APA violent video game task force*

In response to such findings, the APA urged the ESRB to further reflect on violent material in video games. The ESRB rejected this request. It thought the task force's solutions were incorrect. However, an ESRB spokesperson said, "We have spoken with the APA members in the past and are open to continuing a dialogue with them to better understand their viewpoint."[24]

A 2018 research project led by Simone Kühn from the Max Planck Institute for Human Development is providing valuable resources for the pro-gaming community. Kühn's longitudinal study was performed to evaluate the long-term effects of violent video games on levels of aggression. A longitudinal research study is accomplished by observing and gathering data from the same research subjects over

Some video games that are appropriate for children still have elements of violence. Parents can play games with their children to understand the types of violence in games.

an extended period of time. Ninety participants were involved in Kühn's study. The average age of the participants was twenty-eight. The participants were placed into three categories. The first group played the violent game *Grand Theft Auto V*. The second played a nonviolent game, *The Sims 3*, in which players control the everyday lives of virtual people. The third group did not play video games. The participants in the two groups who were assigned video games were asked to play the games on a daily basis for two months.

Before and after the two months of heavy game use, the participants were asked to complete a variety of tests. These tests evaluated various behavior traits, including aggression, sexist attitudes, empathy, sensation seeking, boredom proneness, risk taking, and levels of depression or anxiety. There were no observable changes in any of the categories between the pre-test and the post-test. There were no statistically significant differences between the violent-title gamers, non-violent game players, and the group that played no video games at all. The research team concluded that these findings provide strong evidence that violent video games do not play a significant role in real-world problems. However, secondary findings of this study did suggest that there are short-lived increases of aggression that last less than fifteen minutes following gameplay. The researchers contend this is not the type of increased aggression that sparks permanent behavioral changes. While more research is needed, this study is considered the most comprehensive long-term evaluation of violent video games and behavioral changes.

There is conflicting evidence about the link between real and digital violence. Other research teams have dug deeper into this relationship. One possible link between violent games and real-life violent behavior is the extent to which the game normalizes its extreme content.

DESENSITIZATION

The human brain has the ability to undergo amazing changes. One of these changes involves becoming less sensitive to emotional or shocking stimuli. This process is called desensitization. A person who is desensitized no longer feels fear, anxiety, or guilt after repeated exposure to something that originally caused those feelings. Through several scientific research studies, psychology experts have demonstrated that people can become desensitized to violence through repeated exposure to violent video games.

First-person shooters can desensitize people to violence. Many tie the game's objectives or achievements to doing aggressive things.

In 2016, a study was published about desensitization in the journal *Media Psychology*. It took five days to complete. The experiment's participants played alternative versions of a violent video game. Each participant was randomly assigned a gameplay character for the first four days. The character was either a United Nations soldier or a terrorist soldier. On the fifth day, every participant was given the role of a terrorist character in a completely different game. By the end of the study, the researchers noted significant behavioral changes.

For some of the participants, there was a feeling a guilt early in the study when given the role as the terrorist soldier. To advance in the game, they were forced to commit violent acts against innocent virtual characters. After repeated exposure to this role, the feelings of guilt diminished or were no longer noted. During the fifth day's gaming experience, the feeling of guilt was greatly reduced even though the game and situation were entirely different. This study showed evidence that exposure to violent video games desensitizes gamers to future video game experiences.

A 2006 study at Iowa State University tracked physical changes during exposure to violent media. Each participant had baseline measurements of heart rate and other bodily responses. There were no significant differences between the participants in these initial measurements. After the baseline testing, participants were randomly assigned one of eight different video games to play. Four of the games were violent. They were *Carmageddon*, *Duke Nukem*, *Mortal Kombat*, and *Future Cop*. The other four games were not violent. They were *Glider Pro*, *3D Pinball*, *3D Munch Man*, and *Tetra Madness*.

After gaming for twenty minutes, the subjects were monitored for an additional five minutes. Then, all participants were required to watch a ten-minute video that featured courtroom outbursts, police confrontations, shootings, and prison fights. Heart rates and other physical responses were recorded throughout the viewing. There was a substantial difference in these responses. Those who played the violent video games displayed a significantly lower heart rate during the video viewing. "It appears that individuals who play violent video games habituate or 'get used to' all the violence and eventually become physiologically numb to it," said project researcher Nicholas Carnagey.[25] He added, "The results demonstrate that playing violent video games, even for just 20 minutes, can cause people to become less physiologically aroused by real violence."[26]

The research team was troubled by what these findings might mean for society. Project leader Professor Craig Anderson stated, "In short, the modern entertainment media landscape could accurately be described as an effective systematic violence desensitization tool. Whether modern societies want this to continue is largely a public policy question, not an exclusively scientific one."[27]

A two-part research study from the University of Missouri tracked video game use and changes to the brain. The participants in the study were separated into two groups that played either violent or non-violent games. The violent games included the popular titles in the Call of Duty and Grand Theft Auto series. After twenty-five minutes of gameplay, the participants were shown both neutral images, such as a person riding a bike, and violent images. Brain responses were recorded during the image viewing session. Those who played the violent games had a smaller brain response to the violent images. Those who reported routine use of violent video games before the study had an especially low response to the violent images.

The second portion of this study measured aggression levels after playing the violent games. Following the twenty-five minutes of gaming, participants competed against each other in a task. The winner had the opportunity to blast a noise at the loser. The volume of the noise was controllable by the winner. Those who played the violent video games were more likely to blast a significantly louder noise than the non-violent game users. The research team interpreted this as a higher level of aggression.

The study found that the participants with smaller brain responses to violent photos in the first portion of the study matched the more aggressive participants in the second part. University of Missouri psychology professor Bruce Bartholow stated, "Many researchers have believed that becoming desensitized to violence leads to increased human aggression. Until our study, however, this causal association had never been demonstrated experimentally."[28]

LEARNING AND REWARDING VIOLENCE

Exploring how video games are won and lost is critical for understanding why some believe gamers are faster to resort to violence in the real world. Some critics worry that the way video games are designed teaches people to become more violent. Using a reward system is a powerful way to encourage someone to continue a behavior. In violent video games, the player receives rewards and wins the game by inflicting maximum damage on the enemy. Some people believe that video games are teaching humans to solve problems with violence by rewarding them for violent behavior. Part of the answer was first discovered by observing the behavior of dogs.

In the early twentieth century, Russian scientist Ivan Pavlov began studying the behavior of dogs. Every time he brought out food for the dogs, he rang a bell. Knowing that the dinner time was near, the dogs began to drool. Eventually, if Pavlov wanted his dogs to drool, he only needed to ring the bell. Over time, the dogs had associated the ringing of the bell with food. Pavlov discovered that animals, including humans, learn behavior unintentionally no matter how unnatural or irrational it seems. This process is known as classical conditioning.

KICKING THE HABIT

People can become addicted to playing video games. They may become conditioned to need the rewards that video games provide. But helping people to end their habit often has unwelcomed side effects. Psychologist Kimberly Young states, "They become angry, violent, or depressed. If [parents] take away the computer, their child sits in the corner and cries, refuses to eat, sleep, or do anything." There are now treatment centers specializing in curing video game addictions.

There are warning signs of video game addiction. According to the Center for On-line Addiction, signs of gaming addiction include: playing for an increased amount of time, thinking about games during other everyday activities, using games to escape from real-life problems, lying to family and friends about gaming habits, and feeling irritable when trying to lessen the amount of gaming. Young does not see the problem getting better.

Quoted in Sherry Rauh, "Video Game Addiction No Fun," WebMD, n.d. www.webmd.com.

Another type of trained learning is called operant conditioning. Psychologist B.F. Skinner is considered the father of operant conditioning. The theory of operant conditioning includes the belief that behaviors that are reinforced by a response are more likely to be repeated. This response is called an operant. Skinner believed there are three types of operants: neutral, reinforcement, and punishment. A neutral operant is a response that does not increase or decrease the probability that the action will be repeated. Reinforcement increases the probability that the action is repeated. Punishment decreases the probability of the action being repeated. Both classical and operant conditioning techniques are used in violent video games.

Before the age of seven, children have a difficult time differentiating between what is real and what is not. Many people believe violent video games are especially dangerous for children because of the effects of classical and operant conditioning. Gamers play to win. They do nearly anything to advance and ultimately achieve victory. In the Grand Theft Auto games, the character steals, sells drugs, and kills police officers. These acts are rewarded with increases in digital money and health. Acts that would land you in prison in the real world are rewarded and even required for continued gameplay.

The game isn't real, but the person playing the game is real. They may be conditioned to associate violence with rewards.

University of Notre Dame psychologist Darcia Narvaez believes a child's developing brain is negatively affected by exposure to violent video games. She writes, "When you play a violent video game, you practice it over and over . . . and what you practice is what you become."[29] Narvaez believes the brain reacts in a primitive way during gameplay. The player is conditioned to feel pleasure by committing cruel acts. She argues these rewards decrease the empathy for people suffering in the real world. Narvaez claims, "Research shows that normal kids immersed in such games develop 'game brain,' in which those more thoughtful parts hardly operate at all."[30]

A significant critique of violent video games is that they have potential to teach bad behaviors. However, a research study from the University of York suggests that

> **"When you play a violent video game, you practice it over and over . . . and what you practice is what you become."** [29]
>
> —*Darcia Narvaez, psychologist*

As video game technology gets more realistic, so does the violence. People may have a hard time differentiating between video game violence and violence in the real world.

is actually not the case. Some of the research that portrays violent video gaming as a harmful activity is partially based upon a model of learning called priming.

Priming occurs when a person is repeatedly exposed to concepts such as violence in video games. With increased exposure, the concept becomes easier to use in the real world. The University of York research team designed an expansive study that sought answers about priming and violent video games. The study included more than 3,000 participants.

In one portion of the study, the research subjects played a game where they either controlled a car avoiding crashes with trucks or a mouse avoiding capture by a cat. Following the game, the players were shown various images such as a bus or a dog. The subjects were asked to describe the image as either an animal or a vehicle. University of York researcher Dr. David Zendle said, "If players are 'primed' through immersing themselves in the concepts of the game, they should be able to categorize the objects associated with this game more quickly in the real world once the game had concluded."[31]

However, the data concluded that significant priming did not occur in these gamers. Dr. Zendle adds, "Participants who played a car-themed game were no quicker at categorizing vehicle images, and indeed in some cases their reaction time was significantly slower."[32] The study suggests that gamers are not applying concepts from video games to the real world. However, the study only used adult participants. Researchers stated that "more work is needed to understand whether a different effect is evident in children players."[33]

A second study by this research team reviewed the effects of increasingly realistic violence. The experiment compared the reactions in gamers from playing two violent games. One game used a technique called ragdoll physics, while the other did not. Ragdoll physics is a design strategy that causes the video game characters to move in the same manner as real people when they collapse after being injured or killed. Such physics can make a game's graphics seem more realistic.

> "Participants who played a car-themed game were no quicker at categorizing vehicle images, and indeed in some cases their reaction time was significantly slower." [32]
>
> —Dr. David Zendle, University of York

After subjects played the two games, they were asked to complete a word-association activity. Researchers expected that if priming truly occurred, the gamers who played the more realistic violent game would choose more violent words in the activity. This did not appear to be the case. Dr. Zendle states, "There was no difference in priming between the game that employed 'ragdoll physics' and the game that didn't. The findings suggest that there is no link between these kinds of realism in games and the kind of effects that video games are commonly thought to have on their players."[34]

The negative consequences of violent video gaming are still being debated and researched. Violent video games don't just have potentially bad outcomes. Meanwhile, other studies show violent video games have positive effects on a person's mental health and cognitive abilities.

VIOLENCE PROVIDES RELIEF?

Psychologists believe it is important and healthy to release, or let go, of strong emotions. The process of getting relief is called catharsis. For many people, playing violent video games is a source of catharsis.

Buddhist monks meditate to control their emotions. Typically monks aren't associated with violent video games, but Ogyen Trinley Dorje is an exception. As of 2018, he is the Karmapa, which is the religious leader of a sub-school of Buddhism known as Karma Kagyu. When he needs stress release, the Karmapa turns to an unlikely source. He said, "If I'm having some negative thoughts or negative feelings, video games are one way in which I can release that energy in the context of the illusion of the game. I feel better afterwards."[35]

One doesn't have to be a spiritual leader to obtain positive mental health benefits from video games. There is evidence that

When children play with toys, conflict can arise that feels unsafe. They can face similar experiences in a virtual world.

shows children benefit emotionally from playing violent video games. In violent games, the gamer is placed into fear-inducing or frustrating situations. While some parents see this experience as troubling, it has potential benefits.

In video games, children learn how to face the situations in a safe manner. Psychologist Dr. Peter Gray notes, "In play, children learn that they can experience these emotions and can subsequently calm themselves. They don't have to panic or have a tantrum."[36] Conversely, Dr. Gray believes if children are protected from these hostile digital environments, they are less capable of responding to real stresses appropriately.

IN GOOD HANDS

Coordinating the on-screen action of violent video games requires good hand-eye coordination. This is the way that hands and eyes work together to control movement and decisions. While some people may be born naturally more coordinated, research has shown this skill can be improved by routine video game use. This enhanced hand-eye coordination has already translated into real-world success.

A study performed by Dr. JC Rosser demonstrated that surgeons who played video games routinely were significantly faster and more accurate than those who didn't. The study also showed that surgeons playing video games just prior to surgery was especially beneficial for their patients. Patients who spend less time in surgery receive less anesthesia. Longer anesthesia sessions have been correlated with higher risks of complications including heart attack and pneumonia.

A study published in *Social Psychiatry and Psychiatric Epidemiology* supports Dr. Gray's beliefs. The 2016 study of children ages six to eleven concluded that the children who played more than five hours of video games a week experienced fewer mental health difficulties than those who played for less time or who played no video games at all.

Dr. Christopher Ferguson of Texas A&M University presented research that also supports the stress relief benefits of violent video games. He argues that violent games help manage the mood of young gamers. In his research published in *European Psychologist*, Dr. Ferguson writes:

> In this study, 103 young adults were given a frustration task and then randomized to play no game, a non-violent game, a violent game with good versus evil theme, or a violent game in which they played 'the bad guy.' The results suggest that

*violent games reduce depression and hostile feelings in
players through mood management.*[37]

According to Concordia University, managing stress leads to a
long list of positive health benefits. Some of these effects include
a decreased incidence of heart disease, lower risk of diabetes,
a stronger immune system, and decreased risk of cancer. While
gaming is only one method of stress relief, it has potential to be a
healthy endeavor.

A study from the University of Rochester found that violent video
games might also make gamers better at learning. Researcher and
professor Daphne Bavelier said, "Prior research . . . has shown that
action gamers excel at many tasks. In this new study, we show they
excel because they are better learners. And they become better
learners by playing the fast-paced action games."[38]

The study compared subjects who played no games versus
games such as those in the Call of Duty series. Those who played
the violent titles were better at learning new tasks that researchers
assigned. A year after the initial assessment, the violent-title gamers
were still more improved at the same tasks than the non-gamers.
Bavelier credits this cognitive superiority to an increased ability to
recognize patterns. Pattern recognition is a common element of
video games.

A faster and healthier mind are just two possible results of violent
video game usage. While some people believe that society as a whole
benefits from controversial games, others view violent games as a
threat to communities.

HOW DOES VIOLENCE IN VIDEO GAMES AFFECT SOCIETY?

The influence of violent video games does not only affect individual gamers. Violent video games cause widespread impacts in many aspects of society, including the military and schools. While some of these effects are potentially negative and hazardous, other violent gaming experiences are helping make communities safer.

TRAINING TACTICS

Systematic desensitization is a legitimate concern of critics of violent video games. However, desensitization to violence is now an important training component for some members of the military. Realistic gaming violence is playing a role in keeping soldiers safe.

For someone who has never gone into a combat zone, it is difficult to imagine the horrors that possibly await them. Many soldiers experience traumatic and graphic violence on routine deployments. The military has sought the help of violent video games to prepare soldiers' minds for warzones. With funding from the US government, University of Southern California psychologist Albert Rizzo and his team created a VR lab that simulates traumatic events. The goal

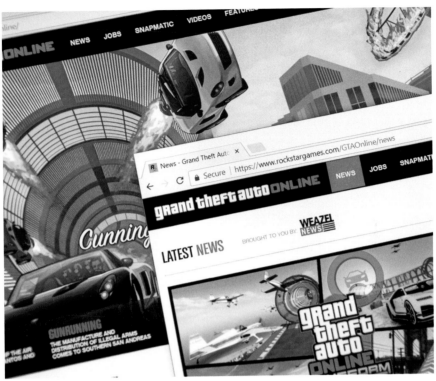

Grand Theft Auto Online *is an online multiplayer game. Players around the world can join teams to kill targets, rob stores, and blow up vehicles.*

of this training is to prepare new recruits for all types of mentally and emotionally strenuous scenarios. "What we want to create is something that pulls at the hearts of people," said Rizzo. He added, "Maybe your action kills an innocent civilian, or you see a guy next to you get shot in the eye with blood spurting out of his face."[39]

The game freezes during the peak stress point of the simulator. A calming character enters the scene and walks the trainee step-by-step through the scenario. This timing is done for an important reason. Rizzo explains that "you want to teach people this stuff when they're in a state of arousal so that they're more likely to access that learning when they're in a similar state."[40]

This type of training builds a characteristic called stress-resilience. Stress-resilience is a form of desensitization to violence. It builds confidence and competence on the battlefield. This resilience has potential to prevent soldiers from freezing or making critical errors that cost lives. Building stress-resilience through VR training also helps a soldier after returning home from a violent deployment.

One hurdle that was difficult for the VR lab team to overcome was making the virtual environment feel real. Brookings Institute defense expert Peter Singer states, "Any military person will tell you that there's a blend of incredible intensity and stress combined with long years of boredom. But is a game going to capture that?"[41] According to Singer,

A DIGITAL ESCAPE

Video games are being used for treatment of soldiers who have been diagnosed with PTSD. When traditional therapy techniques and medications have failed, some of these individuals turn to violent games as an escape from the powerful symptoms.

Retired Army specialist Rob Gibson once loved outdoor activities as a way to unwind from stressful situations. Since a violent deployment to Iraq, Gibson no longer enjoys going outdoors as it creates extreme anxiety. Instead, he finds peace while playing *Counter-Strike*, *Mass Effect* and *Fallout*. Gibson said, "It's kind of nice just because you focus on that other person for like 90 minutes: I'm not Rob with PTSD, I'm that person in the game. I'm very vocal there, calling out which location to go to and stuff like that." While Gibson's gaming sessions weren't prescribed by a physician, many PTSD sufferers report similar successes in managing symptoms by escaping to the digital world.

Quoted in Jake Offenhartz, "How Video Games Are Helping Young Veterans Cope," Complex, November 11, 2016. www.complex.com.

this blurring of lines between real and virtual war can distort how people view a war's true essence. Despite this shortcoming, military VR training is valuable both before and after a deployment.

Simulated violence training provided by the military may have played a role in reducing the incidence of post-traumatic stress disorder (PTSD) soldiers faced following deployments to Iraq and Afghanistan. A 2008 study by the RAND Corporation calculated the rate of PTSD in returning soldiers. Of the 1,938 studied participants who were involved in either the Iraq or Afghanistan wars, the prevalence of PTSD was 13.8 percent. In a separate study called the National Vietnam Veterans Readjustment Study, 30.9 percent of men and 26.9 percent of women who were deployed to the Vietnam War suffered from PTSD.

VR is used in therapy for PTSD sufferers. Even if the game graphics are poor, the virtual environment is a powerful tool. Psychologists believe that leaving some gaps to the imagination is a good thing. It allows the PTSD sufferers to insert their own experiences into the digital realm. Rizzo and his team studied a group of Vietnam veterans in their virtual reality lab. According to Rizzo, "When the patients got out of the [virtual helicopter], a couple of them were describing [enemy soldiers] shooting from the jungle and water buffaloes in the rice paddies. None of that was in the simulation—they had blended in their own experiences."[42]

Rizzo and his colleagues hope pre-deployment stress-resilience training helps reduce the need for PTSD therapy. He also believes it helps returning soldiers transition back into the civilian world. Rizzo states, "That's what our aim is, to make the return home as smooth as possible."[43]

IMPROVING TECHNICAL SKILLS

Besides the emotional and stress-related aspects of VR training, there are experts who believe games have the potential to create soldiers with more technical skills. Dr. Ray Perez is a program manager at the Office of Naval Research's Cognitive Science of Learning Program. According to Perez, "Video game players are far superior . . . in the ability to process things like field of vision, being able to hold digital objects in your memory. They can process information faster."[44]

The average person settles between doing something faster or doing something better in a phenomenon called the speed-accuracy trade-off. Dr. Perez believes gamers can rise above this. He said, "They increase their speed but they don't commit more errors."[45]

> **"They increase their speed but they don't commit more errors."** [45]
>
> —Dr. Ray Perez, program manager at the Office of Naval Research's Cognitive Science of Learning Program

What the research team is trying to determine is whether gamers are capable of applying this unique ability toward specific military skills and techniques.

Military leaders are embracing VR technology for many reasons besides training, practice, and therapy. VR simulators also save money. Simulators are much less dangerous to trainees than field training. The simulators can also target specific cognitive skills that need improvement. Real field equipment is much more fragile and difficult to replace than simulators. VR's benefits will increase as research continues to expand in the field of game-based training.

Training in the VR realm is also used by local law enforcement agencies. Some believe this type of training has potential to decrease the number of police-involved shootings. Learning situations in a practice environment helps decision making in the real world. The decision for police to use deadly force is often a split-second decision. The director of New Jersey's Morris County Public Safety Training Academy, Scott Digiralomo, says, "The question comes down to the decision the officer made, and whether the officer should have used deadly force. A lot of that comes down to decision making."[46]

Digiralomo believes violent virtual training is critical to helping his officers develop decision making skills. The system his academy uses is called VirTra. This state-of-the-art system cost Morris County nearly $300,000. However, the county believes that the cost is worth well-trained police who can make better decisions. A trainee plays through a wide variety of scenarios and receives real-time feedback on whether deciding to pull the trigger was correct or not. While the system does not produce every possible situation an officer may face, Digiralomo asserts his officers are much better off in the community after this VR training.

While opponents believe lives are being ruined by violent video games, researchers and defense experts are focusing on how lives can be improved or saved. Through technical training, situational awareness, and even therapy, violent VR gaming experiences are improving the mindset of the modern soldier and police officer. Stress relief is a benefit of violent gaming available not only to veterans, but to anyone with a gaming system.

Doom *revolutionized the first-person shooter (FPS) genre of video games. Many FPS games are released every year.*

REAL-LIFE VIOLENCE

In 2018, the topic of mass shootings was a hot-button issue. Following high school shootings in Parkland, Florida, and Santa Fe, Texas, the issue dominated front page news. Debates over causes and solutions included gun control, violent media, and mental health concerns. The role violent video games play in mass shootings had already been debated for decades.

Game-inspired violence became a topic of national discussion in 1999 following the Columbine High School shooting in Littleton, Colorado. One of the shooters was Eric Harris. Following the shootings, authorities dug into his game playing past. Harris was discovered to be a fan of the game *Doom*. One of the intriguing features of the original *Doom* was the ability to create custom levels and modifications of weapons and enemies. Some media outlets originally reported that Harris and his accomplice Dylan Klebold created custom maps in *Doom* that mimicked the layout of Columbine. While this was later proven false, people have since created highly accurate maps in *Doom* that resemble the layout of the high school.

Rabbi Abraham Cooper is the Associate Dean of the Simon Wiesenthal Center, a Jewish human rights organization that investigates hateful websites on the internet. Cooper lays some blame for the shootings on *Doom*. He stated, "There's not a question that this was kind of the precursor for what they acted out in real life."[47] In video recordings taken before the shootings, Harris linked the upcoming murders to the game. He says, "It's going to be like *Doom*. Tick, tick, tick, tick . . . Ha! That shotgun is straight out of *Doom*!"[48]

While there are many factors for Harris and Klebold's motivations, victims' families believed violent games made the shooters carry out their murders. In 2001, these families attempted to sue the makers of *Doom* and *Mortal Kombat*. The suit was dismissed in a federal court in 2002.

There have been many school shootings since the Columbine massacre. After every one, questions are raised about whether violent video games played a role in the events. The debate is very personal and emotional for many people.

Parkland shooter Nikolas Cruz was reported to have spent an average of eight to fifteen hours a day playing violent video games. While critics view this as troubling, many doubt it was the root cause for the shootings. Samuel Zeif is a survivor of the Parkland shooting.

He does not see violent video games as the cause of the rampage. Zeif stated, "My friends and I have been playing video games our whole life and never have we ever felt driven or provoked by those actions in those games to do something as horrible as this. I don't think anyone is." He added, "It's a video game. Something happens, you restart. We know that's not how life is."[49]

> **"My friends and I have been playing video games our whole life and never have we ever felt driven or provoked by those actions in those games to do something as horrible as this. I don't think anyone is."**[49]
>
> —*Samuel Zeif, Parkland shooting survivor*

Video game violence isn't only debated in America. In 2016, a shooter in Munich, Germany, took the lives of nine people. An investigation found a history of mental illness, as well as bullying by his peers. Also discovered was the shooter's obsession with the first-person shooter *Counter-Strike*. During the investigation, a sixteen-year-old gamer who had played with the shooter stated, "We always expected something like what happened, but we never thought he could get a gun and then use it."[50]

There are many instances of mass shooters being heavy users of violent video games. The debate rages on while the search for links to real violence continues. Despite the correlation between murderers and video games, this association does not prove a cause.

While opponents of violence in video games continue to be outspoken in their beliefs, there is another side to this story. There any many experts, scientists, and parents who believe violent video games do not cause societal problems. There are some who believe violent video games actually play an important positive role.

VIDEO GAMES AND CRIME

A 2005 essay by University of Southern California professor Henry Jenkins tried to explain why juvenile crime was at a thirty-year low in the United States. He wrote, "Researchers find that people serving time for violent crimes typically consume less media before committing their crimes than the average person in the general population."[51] He saw no link between violent gaming and acts of violent crime.

Villanova and Rutgers University researchers discovered a possible link between violent video games and real-world violence and crime. The results are not what the critics expected. The study published in the APA's journal *Psychology of Popular Media* suggests there is a decrease in violent crimes shortly after violent video games are released for sale to the public. It tracked violent video game sales and acts of violent crime between 2007 and 2011. When video game sales were incredibly high from titles in the Call of Duty and Grand Theft Auto series, rates of crimes such as homicide and aggravated assault decreased. This trend of game sales causing a decreased rate of crime can be described as a negative statistical relationship.

Project co-author Patrick Markey believes this is no coincidence. He notes, "We have taken into account trends in the data. We remove stuff that typically happens, like a spike in murders during summer

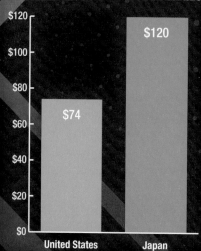

AVERAGE MONEY PER PERSON SPENT ANNUALLY ON VIDEO GAMES

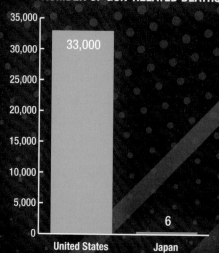

NUMBER OF GUN-RELATED DEATHS

Many experts believe violent video games have no link to gun deaths in the United States. In 2018, psychologist Patrick Markey conducted research that showed that 80 percent of mass shooters were not interested in violent video games. Though critics warn of a connection between video games and gun deaths, Markey states that "the problem is just the science, the data, does not back up that they actually have an effect."

Some experts use worldwide crime rates as evidence against the connection between gun deaths and violent video games. In 2014, gamers in Japan on average spent $120 annually on video games, which was the highest in the world. However, there were only six gun-related deaths in Japan that year. By comparison, gamers in the United States on average spent only $74 a year on video games. However, there were over 33,000 gun-related deaths in the United States.

Another study showed the relationship between gun violence and revenue from video game purchases. The study revealed no correlation between them. The United States was the only country that both purchased a large number of video games and committed a high number of gun-related crimes.

Quoted in Anna Weber, "80 Percent of Mass Shooters Showed No Interest in Video Games, Researcher Says," CBS News, March 8, 2018. www.cbsnews.com.

and high sales of games near the holidays, and it's still negative. To me what is most amazing is that [it] is never positive. It is always statistically negative."[52]

While there are deeper psychological factors that perhaps lead to this decrease, Markey prefers a simpler theory. If a large number of people purchase and play video games shortly after the game's release, they spend more time in front of television or computer screen where there is a lower likelihood of committing a crime. Markey concludes, "In other words, because violent individuals are playing violent video games in their homes, there may be a decrease in violent crime when popular violent video games are released."[53]

Psychologist Dr. Patricia Greenfield believes that moderation is the key to limiting violence. In an opinion piece for the *Miami Herald* she writes, "The answer is that video games can provide an opportunity to practice and learn how to carry out mass murder. . . . But a potential shooter still needs the tools."[54] She does not think the answer is to ban either exclusively. In her opinion, both are considered major risk factors for mass shootings. Greenfield concludes, "So, anything our society can do to decrease these two major risk factors— violent video game play

> **"The answer is that video games can provide an opportunity to practice and learn how to carry out mass murder. . . . But a potential shooter still needs the tools."** [54]
>
> —Dr. Patricia Greenfield, psychologist

and the availability of assault weapons—will also lower our collective risk of mass murder."[55]

A HOSTILE WORLD

Many video games are not a solo activity, with individuals playing alone. Rather, many titles connect people from all over the world through online multiplayer gaming. Even in games with E or E10+ ESRB ratings, unpredictable online interactions can introduce adult content not foreseen by the game's developers.

While the level of violence in the games varies greatly, parents must also consider the multiplayer environment. It is difficult to control the behavior of other players. There are widespread reports of racist, sexist, and homophobic language used between online gamers. Instances of threats of violence or other forms of harassment are cause for concern in the gaming community. Researchers are finding ways to combat this inappropriate conduct, but rude gamers still find ways around default vulgarity filters. One of these researchers is Jeffrey Lin, a cognitive neuroscientist working for Riot Games, the makers of the popular game *League of Legends*. "Everybody you talk to thinks of the internet as this hate-filled place," he says. "Why do we think that's a normal part of gaming experiences?"[56] Lin seeks to find the reasons why a culture of hate and violence often finds its way into the multiplayer gaming community.

Law professor Elizabeth Handsley believes gamers who play violent games develop a negative outlook. This type of thinking leads them to believe that others have bad intentions. With danger around every corner in video games, having that mentality could cause some to believe the same is true in everyday life. Handsley notes:

The number of people that end up behaving violently or aggressively is only ever going to be very small, but the number of people who become desensitized or oversensitive to other people's aggression is going to be greater, and that will have that broader, society-wide effect that we won't necessarily be able to identify. . . . If you have inherent distrust of people, or read aggressive intent into words and actions that might otherwise be quite innocent . . . that's going to have an impact at a societal level.[57]

While there hasn't been a direct scientific link established between video games and acts of real violence, critics argue that games teach a bad lesson. New South Wales police commissioner Andrew Scipione said, "When you see video games that reward behavior, where somebody's murdered . . . what sort of messages are we sending our children?"[58] As a police official, Scipione sees the worst aspects of society and strongly opposes video game violence. He states, "In reality there's no reset button that can bring the player back to life. The real world is not a video game. Game over is game over."[59]

> **"In reality there's no reset button that can bring the player back to life. The real world is not a video game. Game over is game over."** [59]
>
> —*Andrew Scipione, New South Wales police commissioner*

CHAPTER 4

THE FUTURE OF
VIOLENCE IN
VIDEO GAMES

The debate over violence and video games does not appear to be ending soon. Despite a gridlock between critics of violent video games and advocates, there have been key decisions made by powerful forces in society. These decisions will steer the future of violence in video games. One important judgement involved the highest court in the United States.

A SUPREME CHALLENGE

If the lower courts cannot reach a satisfactory ruling on a case, the United States Supreme Court can decide to make a powerfully influential conclusion. Violence and video games is so controversial that it led to a Supreme Court case.

On October 7, 2005, California state legislators passed Assembly Bill 1179. Signed by former Governor Arnold Schwarzenegger, the law prohibited the sale or rental of violent video games to minors. The attorney general defending the bill was Jerry Brown. As written in the law, minors are defined as any person under the age of eighteen. Furthermore, any game that displayed killing, maiming, dismembering,

UNFILTERED VIOLENCE

The software company Valve created a highly successful online gaming platform called Steam. Steam allows gamers to have instant access to a wide variety of games, including violent titles. In 2018, a highly controversial game called *Active Shooter* was due for release. The game is a first-person shooter which is played by rampaging through a school killing students, teachers, and police officers. Following school shootings in Santa Fe, Texas and Parkland, Florida, Steam decided to cancel the game's release. Despite this cancellation, Steam still features titles many people find offensive such as *Kindergarten*, a game in which the principal and janitor kills cartoon students.

Steam has decided to take a new approach to releasing games: allow everything. The organization decided every game will be released except if the content is illegal or was deemed to have been deliberately created to upset people. The organization issued a statement that read, "The Steam store is going to contain something that you hate, and don't think should exist. Unless you don't have any opinions, that's guaranteed to happen."

Quoted in Louis Lucero II, "Steam, After Pulling School Shooter Game, Says It Will Sell Nearly Everything," New York Times, May 29, 2018. www.nytimes.com.

or sexual assault against the image of a human character would have to be marked with the label "18". Individuals or businesses that violated AB-1179 could face a fine up to $1,000. Almost immediately, the video game industry sought to have it overturned. The industry believed the First Amendment rights of all gamers and game creators were violated by this legislation. They fought back in the court system as the Entertainment Merchants Association (EMA).

The first court battle was brought to a California federal district court. The court declared the banning the sale of violent video games was unconstitutional. The state of California took the case further to the US Court of Appeals Ninth Circuit. This court ruled in the same manner as the district court for three reasons. The first reason declared that violence in video games is not considered an obscenity. Therefore, such displays are protected by the First Amendment. Secondly, they did not find the state had a compelling interest in protecting minors from alleged neurological or psychological harm. Lastly, the court declared that even if the state had a compelling interest, the law as written did not do enough to meet their objective.

This ruling did not do enough to satisfy both parties. Upon appeal, the case was accepted to the level of the US Supreme Court. On November 2, 2010, the nine Justices of the Supreme Court heard arguments from both sides. Zackery P. Morazzini argued on behalf of the state of California. Paul M. Smith represented the video gaming industry. The case is known as *Brown v. Entertainment Merchants Association.*

It took the court more than eight months to reach a final ruling. It was decided on June 27, 2011. In an overwhelming seven-to-two decision, the court ruled in favor of the gaming industry. The Supreme Court declared that it is unconstitutional to ban the sales of violent video games to minors. The late Supreme Court Justice Antonin Scalia was a part of the voting majority. Scalia wrote, "Like the protected books, plays and movies that preceded them, video games communicate ideas—and even social messages—through many familiar literary devices . . . and through features distinctive to the medium (such as the player's interaction with the virtual world)."[60]

Justice Clarence Thomas disagreed with the Supreme Court's decision. In his dissent he wrote, "I do not think the First Amendment stretches that far. The practices and beliefs of the founding generation establish that 'the freedom of speech,' as originally understood, does not include a right to speak to minors (or a right of minors to access speech) without going through the minors' parents or guardians."[61]

The US Supreme Court is in Washington, D.C. Supreme Court decisions on cases can have lasting impacts on society.

Nonetheless, the decision was made to protect the right of violent game sales to minors.

This decision gave video games a new designation. Video games, including violent games, were now viewed legally as being in the same category alongside books, plays, and movies. Artistic expression is protected under the right to freedom of speech granted by the Constitution. In his writings, Justice Scalia noted that another form of artwork originally wasn't protected in the way video games are now. In 1915, the Supreme Court unanimously ruled that motion pictures were not worthy of First Amendment protection in the case *Mutual Film Corp. v. Industrial Commission of Ohio*. The Court was fearful of some content in motion pictures. It stated, "They may be used for evil. . . . We cannot regard [the censorship of movies] as beyond the power of government."[62] This ruling allowed states to ban movies and potentially criminally punish those who showed films which contained perceived immoral material. It wasn't until 1952 in the case *Joseph Burstyn, Inc. v. Wilson* that the court decided to reverse the decision to grant movies First Amendment protection.

The court's decision on video games ultimately placed responsibility on parents and guardians. The justices decided it is not the role of government to decide what types of games minors can access. The ESRB ratings system is trusted by parents. With the top-selling games priced near $60, parents are already often involved in the purchase of these games.

The legal system granted parents the right to determine when and if violent games are appropriate for children. There are sometimes unintended consequences for this type of freedom. Some critics believe parents are acting irresponsibly. They believe the problem might not be the games themselves, but at what age the children get them, and how often they are allowed to play them.

ORGANIZATIONS RESPOND TO VIOLENT GAMING

Established in 1871, the NRA is an organization dedicated to protecting Second Amendment rights for citizens of the United States. Since the organization's inception, the NRA has become increasingly involved in the political and social landscape.

The NRA has an extensive history of negative views towards violence in video games. After the shooting at Sandy Hook Elementary School in Newtown, Connecticut, NRA CEO Wayne LaPierre stated, "There exists in this country a callous, corrupt and corrupting shadow industry that sells, and sows violence against its own people."[63] The industry he refers to is the video game industry. During this press conference, LaPierre cited *Bulletstorm*, *Grand Theft Auto*, *Mortal Kombat*, and *Splatterhouse* as examples of corrupting video games.

> "There exists in this country a callous, corrupt and corrupting shadow industry that sells, and sows violence against its own people."[63]
>
> —Wayne LaPierre, National Rifle Association CEO

Despite real guns being used in mass shootings, LaPierre suggested virtual weapons are a greater danger to society. He also finds blame in other forms of media by saying, "We have bloodsoaked films out there like *American Psycho*, *Natural Born Killers*, they're aired on propaganda loops called Splatterdays, and every single day. A thousand music videos portray life as a joke, portray murder as a way of life, and then have the nerve to call it entertainment."[64] LaPierre also suggests people and organizations investing in video game companies share in the blame of real life violence. ESA president Mike Gallagher responded to the NRA criticism. He stated, "We know the

NRA makes those arguments. . . . We will continue to be successful with policy makers as the industry continues to grow."[65]

Despite the Supreme Court ruling, there are still gaming advocacy organizations concerned about the future of the gaming industry. One of these groups is the International Game Developers Association (IGDA). The driving purpose of IGDA is to protect the careers of individuals who create video games. One way the organization accomplishes its mission is by fighting against calls for censorship.

IGDA created the Anti-Censorship and Social Issues committee (ACSI). The ACSI is tasked with reaching out to news outlets, politicians, and other media sources to advocate for the benefits of video games. They also explain to their correspondents the potential dangers of censorship. To make their case, the ACSI committee gathers research from a variety of scientific sources.

In 2013, former Vice President Joe Biden sought answers to mass shootings after the Sandy Hook shooting. He held a meeting at the White House inviting professionals and organizations to weigh in on the topic of violent video games. While IGDA wasn't in attendance, it wrote an open letter to Biden. The letter's author was ACSI head Daniel Greenberg. In defense of violent games, he wrote, "We ask that any new research explore the benefits of violent video games, too. For example, recent research shows a steam-valve effect, in which violent video gameplay helps release stress and aggression before it can lead to violence."[66] There were no significant changes following the meeting, but the vice president encouraged the industry to take steps to improve its image with non-gamers.

Another gaming advocacy group, the ESA, was present during the 2018 White House meeting with President Trump. The ESA wrote:

We discussed the numerous scientific studies establishing that there is no connection between video games and violence, First Amendment protection of video games, and how our industry's rating system effectively helps parents make informed entertainment choices. We appreciate the President's receptive and comprehensive approach to this discussion.[67]

Despite the ESA's positive statement, IGDA still saw the meeting as a threat to the video game industry. On March 7, 2018, IGDA tweeted: "Let's be blunt on video games and gun violence—we will not be used as a scapegoat. The facts are very clear—no study has shown a causal relationship between playing video games and gun violence."[68]

> **"Let's be blunt on video games and gun violence—we will not be used as a scapegoat. The facts are very clear—no study has shown a causal relationship between playing video games and gun violence."** [68]
>
> —IGDA, tweeted statement

Even with ongoing criticism, the video game industry continues to create violent games. Exciting new advances are on the horizon, but some believe the industry has already gone too far. New advancements in gaming technology will cause fresh topics for debate.

VIOLENT GAMING: A NEW FRONTIER

With the incredible success of violent titles, many believe the future of video games is about improving them. Gamers are seeking a more realistic feel through better graphics and faster hardware. New technology is bringing the action closer than ever.

> **"Because the appeal of being immersed in an alternate world isn't the primary gaming motivation for many gamers, these gamers would be unlikely to invest in expensive VR equipment."** [69]
>
> —Nick Yee, head of gaming analytics at Quantic Foundry

While exciting and immersive, many experts feel VR technology is not the future of the gaming industry. Quantic Foundry is a market research company. Its head of gaming analytics, Nick Yee, stated that "Because the appeal of being immersed in an alternate world isn't the primary gaming motivation for many gamers, these gamers would be unlikely to invest in expensive VR equipment."[69] Instead, experts believe that gamers will search for something even more realistic.

Augmented reality (AR) is a significant improvement in realism from VR. AR places computer-generated images on the gamer's camera view screen. Essentially, the gamer views imaginary images in the real-world environment. AR became widely popular in 2016 with the release of *Pokémon Go*. This title had gamers roaming their neighborhoods in search of simulated creatures.

In Pokémon Go, *people can catch Pokémon and train them to fight. Items and power-ups can be found at community buildings such as churches and schools.*

While most commonly applied on smartphones or tablets, the creators of Google Glass, Microsoft HoloLens, and Magic Leap Lightware hope to capitalize on a gamer's desire to enhance reality. The US Army is looking strongly at AR as an improved training technology. Instead of being limited by a VR environment, soldiers will be able to train indoors or outdoors. AR is capable of simulating many types of terrain, weather conditions, and weapons. Soldiers testing this new equipment reported feeling uneasy when seeing a simulated life-size helicopter flying around and shooting missiles at them, even though they understood it wasn't real. Even casual users might soon find themselves in frightening AR-enabled scenarios. A demo released by developer Abhishek Singh featured a creepy character that the AR user sees crawling out of the television. The figure chases the gamer around the corner and down the hall.

EVERYTHING IN MODERATION

Studies have shown violent games are often extremely addicting. While research has demonstrated both positive and negative consequences of gaming, overuse has become a problem. In 2018, the World Health Organization began recognizing a condition called gaming disorder.

Young people might be especially at risk for gaming disorder. The region of the brain responsible for self-control is called the pre-frontal cortex. It is not fully developed in humans until the late twenties. But restricting access is not viewed as a realistic solution. Stanford education assistant professor Antero Garcia stated, "If you have a lot of kids who are playing *Fortnite*, then that seems like a real opportunity to think about the kinds of connections you can make."[70] These connections may include modeling real-life scenarios such as school or chores after video games.

The future of violent video game research may be focused on digging deeper into the games' underlying messages. "Turn it into an intellectual enterprise," says Garcia.[71] He believes having young people communicate the reasons why they play shooting games such as *Fortnite* can unlock answers about violent games' deeper meanings. Rather than letting young people simply mash buttons, Garcia encourages asking questions. Some of the questions include:

> What kinds of things do they think they're learning or not
> learning from it? . . . What are the representations of men

People can analyze the content in violent video games. They can study how this violence impacts society.

and women? Who voices the characters and do those racialize them in any kind of way?[72]

Answers to these questions potentially lead to methods of separating the positive aspects of violent video games from the negative.

WHEN DOES VIOLENCE GO TOO FAR?

To stand out from the competition, many game developers have pushed the envelope of extreme violence. There are several violent games inspired by real life tragedies. In the game *Super Columbine*

Massacre RPG!, the gamer plays as Eric Harris and Dylan Klebold as they reenact the Columbine High School shooting. Traffic Software's *JFK: Reloaded* allows gamers to recreate the 1963 presidential assassination of John F. Kennedy. There are many who are still traumatized from these events.

Even some popular titles make gamers uncomfortable. In *Call of Duty: Modern Warfare 2*, the level "No Russian" has the gamer murder dozens of innocent civilians in an airport. However, the developers added an opt-out screen that allows gamers to skip the controversial level without penalty. If players opt in, they do not have to fire any bullets. One of the game's developers, Mohammad Alavi, stated, "The fact that I got the player to hesitate . . . and consider his actions before he pulled that trigger—that makes me feel very accomplished."[73]

Grand Theft Auto V has a level that forces the gamer to torture an enemy using a variety of gruesome tactics. This scene cannot be skipped. It had real victims of torture outraged. "Rockstar [Games] has crossed a line by effectively forcing people to . . . perform a series of unspeakable acts if they want to achieve success in the game," said the Freedom from Torture organization's chief executive, Keith Best.[74]

> **"Rockstar [Games] has crossed a line by effectively forcing people to . . . perform a series of unspeakable acts if they want to achieve success in the game."** [74]
>
> —Keith Best, chief executive of Freedom from Torture

While some people can look past realistic blood and gore, many believe mimicking real-life tragedies and forcing gamers to act especially cruel is morally unacceptable. The Parents Television Council believes that the future of video game sales needs to change. "Video game industry representatives . . . must surely be aware that kids are playing them despite whatever their intentions might be," says PTC program director Melissa Henson.[75] *Mortal Kombat* co-creator Ed Boon said, "Just like a Martin Scorsese film is an R-rated film, with M-rated games, the intention is to design it for someone who has matured, so to speak, not a young, impressionable person."[76]

More studies are needed to examine the effects of violent video games. Researchers are searching for differences in desensitization across cultures. In 2017, a study lead by professor Craig Andersen confirmed that violent media use was "positively and significantly related to aggressive behavior in all countries."[77] Researcher Douglas Gentile stated, "That's not to say media violence deserves special attention, but that it should be considered as seriously as other risk factors such as coming from a broken home. What matters most, however, is not any single risk factor, but how they can combine to increase the risk of aggression."[78]

For gamers and the gaming industry to thrive in the future, balance is critical. Playing violent video games for a moderated number of hours may unlock the benefits of gaming without creating disorders. Gaming developers view shooting games as a key to success, but their critics become more vocal when they cross especially offensive lines. As video games become more and more realistic, the debate over violent games has no end in sight. Moderation from both sides might offer the solutions for compromise.

SOURCE NOTES

INTRODUCTION: A WORLD OF VIOLENCE

1. Jordyn Phelps, "Trump Turns Spotlight on Violent Video Games in Wake of Parkland Shootings," *ABC News*, March 8, 2018. www.abcnews.go.com.

2. Quoted in Rick Nauert, "Negative Effects of Violent Video Games May Build over Time," *Psych Central*, n.d. www.psychcentral.com.

3. Quoted in Luke Barnes, "'Professor of Killology' at NRA Convention Blames Violent Video Games for Mass Shootings," *ThinkProgress*, May 5, 2018. www.thinkprogress.org.

4. Quoted in Lisa Bowen, "Video Game Play May Provide Learning, Health, Social Benefits, Review Finds," *Monitor on Psychology, American Psychological Association*, February 2014. www.apa.org.

5. Quoted in John Patti, "The Level of Violence in Video Games," *Wbal.com*, April 23, 2018. www.wbal.com.

CHAPTER 1: WHAT IS VIOLENCE IN VIDEO GAMES?

6. Quoted in Luke Plunkett, "Death Race, the World's First Scandalous Video Game," *Kotaku,* February 28, 2012. www.kotaku.com.

7. Quoted in Plunkett, "Death Race, the World's First Scandalous Video Game."

8. Quoted in Rob Crossley, "Mortal Kombat: Violent Game That Changed Video Games Industry," *BBC News,* June 2, 2014. www.bbc.com.

9. Quoted in Crossley, "Mortal Kombat: Violent Game That Changed Video Games Industry."

10. Quoted in Crossley, "Mortal Kombat: Violent Game That Changed Video Games Industry."

11. Quoted in Crossley, "Mortal Kombat: Violent Game That Changed Video Games Industry."

12. Quoted in Crossley, "Mortal Kombat: Violent Game That Changed Video Games Industry."

13. Quoted in Keith Stuart, "22 Years on, Doom Retains the Ability to Shock," *Eurogamer,* July 7, 2015. www.eurogamer.net.

14. Quoted in Aernout, "GTA V Sales Reach 95 Million Units, Publisher Take Two Interactive Confirms," *Wccftech*, May 17, 2018. www.wccftech.com.

15. Quoted in Michael Rundle, "Death and Violence 'Too Intense' in VR, Developers Admit," *WIRED*, October 28, 2015, www.wired.co.uk.

16. Quoted in Sarah E. Needleman, "Should Parents Play Videogames with Their Children?" *Wall Street Journal,* September 10, 2015. www.wsj.com.

17. Quoted in "U.S. House and Senate Leaders Urge Parents to Check the Ratings When Purchasing Video Games for Holiday Gifts," *Business Wire,* November 22, 2004. www.businesswire.com.

18. Quoted in ESRB, "What Others Have to Say about the ESRB Rating System," *ESRB*, n.d. www.esrb.org.

19. Quoted in "US Video Game Industry Revenue Reaches $36 Billion in 2017," *The Entertainment Software Association*, January 18, 2018. www.theesa.com.

20. Quoted in "US Video Game Industry Revenue Reaches $36 Billion in 2017."

21. "Call of Duty: WWII." *ESRB*, n.d. www.esrb.org.

CHAPTER 2: HOW DOES VIOLENCE IN VIDEO GAMES AFFECT THE BRAIN AND BODY?

22. Quoted in Associated Press, "Former Surgeon General Dies," *Politico,* August 6, 2014. www.politico.com.

23. Quoted in Alexandra Sifferlin, "Violent Video Games Are Linked to Aggression, Study Says," *Time,* August 17, 2015. www.time.com.

24. Quoted in Anita Busch, "Video Game Ratings Board Says No Changes Coming After Doctor's Group Links Violent Vidgames to Aggression," *Deadline,* August 20, 2015. www.deadline.com.

25. Quoted in Rick Nauert, "Video Games Desensitize to Real Violence," *Psych Central,* July 28, 2006.

26. Quoted in Nauert, "Video Games Desensitize to Real Violence."

27. Quoted in Nauert, "Video Games Desensitize to Real Violence."

28. Quoted in "Violent Video Games Reduce Brain Response to Violence and Increase Aggressive Behavior, University of Missouri Study Finds," *MU News Bureau, University of Missouri,* May 25, 2011. www.munews.missouri.edu.

29. Quoted in "ND Expert: Violent Video Games Link Killing to Rewards, Keep Kids' 'Primitive Brain' in Charge," *Notre Dame News, University of Notre Dame,* November 2, 2010. www.news.nd.edu.

30. Quoted in "ND Expert: Violent Video Games Link Killing to Rewards, Keep Kids' 'Primitive Brain' in Charge."

31. Quoted in University of York, "No Evidence to Support Link Between Violent Video Games and Behavior," *ScienceDaily,* January 16, 2018. www.sciencedaily.com.

32. Quoted in University of York, "No Evidence to Support Link Between Violent Video Games and Behavior."

33. Quoted in University of York, "No Evidence to Support Link Between Violent Video Games and Behavior."

34. Quoted in University of York, "No Evidence to Support Link Between Violent Video Games and Behavior."

35. Quoted in Griffin McElroy, "Buddhist Leader Says Video Games Are Cathartic," *Engadget,* September 9, 2009. www.engadget.com.

36. Peter Gray, "Benefits of Play Revealed in Research on Video Gaming," *Psychology Today,* March 27, 2018, www.psychologytoday.com.

37. Quoted in "Violent Video Games Help Relieve Stress, Depression, Says TAMIU Professor," *The International U, Texas A&M International University,* June 17, 2010. www.tamiu.edu.

38. Quoted in Michael Casey, "Could Playing Video Games Make You Smarter?" *CBS News,* November 12, 2014. www.cbsnews.com.

CHAPTER 3: HOW DOES VIOLENCE IN VIDEO GAMES AFFECT SOCIETY?

39. Quoted in Jeremy Hsu, "For the U.S. Military, Video Games Get Serious," *LiveScience,* August 19, 2010. www.livescience.com.

40. Quoted in Hsu, "For the U.S. Military, Video Games Get Serious."

41. Quoted in Hsu, "For the U.S. Military, Video Games Get Serious."

42. Quoted in Hsu, "For the U.S. Military, Video Games Get Serious."

43. Quoted in Hsu, "For the U.S. Military, Video Games Get Serious."

44. Quoted Sarah Sicard, "Video Games Actually Make You a Better Soldier," *Task & Purpose,* August 23, 2016. www.taskandpurpose.com.

45. Quoted in Sicard, "Video Games Actually Make You a Better Soldier."

46. Quoted in Issie Lapowsky, "The Virtual Reality Sim That Helps Teach Cops When to Shoot," *Wired*, March 30, 2015. www.wired.com.

47. Quoted in Kevin Simpson and Jason Blevins. "Did Harris Preview Massacre on Doom?," *Denver Post Online,* May 4, 1999. www.extras.denverpost.com.

48. Quoted in Nancy Gibbs and Timothy Roach, "The Columbine Tapes," *Time*, December 20, 1999. www.content.time.com.

49. Quoted in Daniel Arkin, "Here's What We Know About the Links Between Video Games and Violence," *NBC News*, March 2, 2018. www.nbcnews.com.

50. Quoted in Tim Hume, "Munich Gunman Planned Attack for a Year, Officials Say," *CNN*, July 24, 2016. www.cnn.com.

51. Quoted in Maya Salam and Liam Stack, "Do Video Games Lead to Mass Shootings? Researchers Say No," *New York Times,* February 23, 2018. www.nytimes.com.

52. Quoted in Colin Campbell, "Do Violent Video Games Actually Reduce Real-World Crime?" *Polygon*, September 12, 2014. www.polygon.com.

53. Quoted in Campbell, "Do Violent Video Games Actually Reduce Real-World Crime?"

54. Patricia Marks Greenfield, "Violent Video Games and Assault Weapons Can Turn into a Lethal Combination," *Miami Herald*, March 15, 2018. www.miamiherald.com.

55. Greenfield, "Violent Video Games and Assault Weapons Can Turn into a Lethal Combination."

56. Quoted in Brendan Maher, "Can a Video Game Company Tame Toxic Behaviour?" *Nature News*, March 30, 2016. www.nature.com.

57. Elle Hunt, "Police Chief Warns Against Violent Video Games That Reward Rape and Murder." *Guardian,* July 18, 2016. www.theguardian.com.

58. Hunt, "Police Chief Warns Against Violent Video Games That Reward Rape and Murder."

59. Hunt, "Police Chief Warns Against Violent Video Games That Reward Rape and Murder."

CHAPTER 4: THE FUTURE OF VIOLENCE IN VIDEO GAMES

60. Quoted in Seth Schiesel, "Supreme Court Has Ruled; Now Games Have a Duty," *New York Times*, June 28, 2011. www.nytimes.com.

61. Quoted in Griffin McElroy, "Supreme Court's Brown v. EMA Opinions: A Digest," *Engadget*, June 27, 2011. www.engadget.com.

62. "Mutual Film Corp. v. Industrial Comm'n of Ohio, 236 U.S. 230 (1915)," *Justia Law*, www.supreme.justia.com.

63. Quoted in Ben Hallman, "NRA Fingers Gun Violence Scapegoat," *Huffington Post*, December 12, 2012. www.huffingtonpost.com.

64. Quoted in Griffin McElroy, "National Rifle Association Exec Blames Video Games for 'Selling Violence' to Children," *Polygon*, December 21, 2012. www.polygon.com.

65. Quoted in Chris Morris, "Video Game Trade Group President Takes On NRA Over Gun Violence," *Fortune*, June 11, 2018. www.fortune.com.

66. Quoted in Jeff Grubb, "Game Developer Association to Biden: 'We Welcome More Evidence-Based Research,'" *VentureBeat*, January 10, 2013. www.venturebeat.com.

67. Quoted in Grubb, "Game Developer Association to Biden."

68. Quoted in Grubb, "Game Developer Association to Biden."

69. Quoted in Patrick Stafford, "What Will the Game Industry Look Like in Five Years?," *Polygon*, November 14, 2017. www.polygon.com.

70. Quoted in Julia James, "Stanford Experts Provide Guidance for How Parents and Teachers Can Navigate the Fortnite Craze," *Stanford Graduate School of Education, Stanford University*, May 4, 2018. www.ed.stanford.edu.

71. Quoted in James, "Stanford Experts Provide Guidance for How Parents and Teachers Can Navigate the Fortnite Craze."

72. Quoted in James, "Stanford Experts Provide Guidance for How Parents and Teachers Can Navigate the Fortnite Craze."

73. Quoted in Patrick Klepek, "That Time Call of Duty Let You Shoot Up an Airport," *Kotaku,* October 23, 2015. www.kotaku.com.

74. Quoted in Alex Hern, "Grand Theft Auto 5 Under Fire for Graphic Torture Scene," *Guardian,* September 18, 2013. www.theguardian.com.

75. Quoted in Mike Snider, "These Are the Video Games the White House Played in Its Meeting on Game Violence," *USA Today,* March 8, 2018. www.usatoday.com.

76. Quoted in Ryan Smith, "Has Mortal Kombat Finally Gone Too Far?" *Chicago Reader*, April 9, 2015. www.chicagoreader.com.

77. Quoted in "Cross-Cultural Study Strengthens Link between Media Violence and Aggressive Behavior," *News Service, Iowa State University*, April 11, 2017. www.news.iastate.edu.

78. Quoted in "Cross-Cultural Study Strengthens Link between Media Violence and Aggressive Behavior."

FOR FURTHER RESEARCH

BOOKS

Gloria G. Adams, *Violent Video Games and Society*. New York: Greenhaven Publishing, 2018.

Dustin Hansen, *Game On! Video Game History from Pong and Pac-Man to Mario, Minecraft, and More*. New York: Fiewel and Friends, 2016.

Andrea C. Nakaya, *Are Video Games Harmful?* San Diego, CA: ReferencePoint Press, 2017.

Ashley Strehle Hartman, *Youth and Video Games*. San Diego, CA: ReferencePoint Press, 2019.

Erika Wittekind, *Violence As Entertainment: Why Aggression Sells*. Mankato, MN: Compass Point Books, 2012.

INTERNET SOURCES

Kyle Orland, "Two Months of Daily *GTA* Causes 'No Significant Changes' in Behavior," *Ars Technica*, March 15, 2018. www.arstechnica.com.

Jordyn Phelps, "Trump Turns Spotlight on Violent Video Games in Wake of Parkland Shootings," *ABC News*, March 8, 2018. www.abcnews.go.com.

Maya Salam and Liam Stack, "Do Video Games Lead to Mass Shootings? Researchers Say No," *New York Times*, February 23, 2018. www.nytimes.com.

"A Timeline of Video Game Controversies," *National Coalition Against Censorship*, n.d. www.ncac.org.

RELATED ORGANIZATIONS AND WEBSITES

American Psychological Association

750 First St. NE
Washington, D.C. 20002-4242
public.affairs@apa.org
www.apa.org

The American Psychological Association (APA) is the largest scientific and professional organization of psychologists in the United States.

Entertainment Merchants Association

16530 Ventura Blvd., Suite 400
Encino, CA 91436-4551
www.entmerch.org

The mission of the Entertainment Merchants Association (EMA) is to promote the interests of those engaged in the sale, rental, and licensed reproduction of entertainment software, such as motion pictures, video games, and sound recordings.

Entertainment Software Association

601 Massachusetts Ave. NW, Suite 300
Washington, D.C. 20001
esa@theESA.com
www.theesa.com

The Entertainment Software Association (ESA) is a US association dedicated to serving the needs of companies that publish video games.

Entertainment Software Ratings Board

317 Madison Ave., 22nd Floor
New York, NY 10017
www.esrb.org

The Entertainment Software Rating Board (ESRB) is the self-regulatory body that assigns ratings for video games and apps.

INDEX

INDEX CONTINUED

IMAGE CREDITS

Cover: © David Grossman/Alamy

4: © Taner Muhlis Karaguzel/Shutterstock Images

5 (top): © davidsmith520/Shutterstock Images

5 (bottom): © PongMoji/iStockphoto

7: © Nicole S Glass/Shutterstock Images

11: © Taner Muhlis Karaguzel/Shutterstock Images

12: © ilbusca/iStockphoto

16: © F-Stop boy/Shutterstock Images

24: © Wachiwit/Shutterstock Images

28: © PeopleImages/iStockphoto

30: © Dejan Stanic Micko/Shutterstock Images

36: © mikkelwilliam/iStockphoto

39: © Zabavna/Shutterstock Images

43: © dennizn/Shutterstock Images

48: © breakermaximus/iStockphoto

52: © Red Line Editorial

59: © davidsmith520/Shutterstock Images

65: © PongMoji/iStockphoto

67: © Creatista/Shutterstock Images

ABOUT THE AUTHOR

John L. Hakala is a freelance writer from Minnesota. Before pursuing a life of writing, he was a nuclear medicine technologist, and he has published research in the *Journal of Nuclear Medicine Technology*. He currently travels with his wife, Heidi. John is the chief contributor for the blog *Liberty by Choice*.